Author:
Cath Senker has written around 160 children's educational books. She is the author of several titles on health topics, including healthy eating and harmful substances.

Series creator:
David Salariya was born in Dundee, Scotland. He has illustrated a wide range of books and has created and designed many new series for publishers in the UK and overseas. David established The Salariya Book Company in 1989. He lives in Brighton, England, with his wife, illustrator Shirley Willis, and their son, Jonathan.

Artists:
Alexandre Affonso, Bryan Beach, Jared Green, Sam Bridges, and Shutterstock.

Editor:
Nick Pierce

PAPER FROM SUSTAINABLE FORESTS

Published in Great Britain in 2019 by
The Salariya Book Company Ltd
25 Marlborough Place, Brighton BN1 1UB

Library of Congress Cataloging-in-Publication Data

Names: Senker, Cath, author. | Affonso, Alexandre, illustrator. | Beach, Bryan, illustrator.
Title: The science of medical technology : from humble syringes to lifesaving robots / written by Cath Senker ; [artists, Alexandre Affonso, Bryan Beach].
Description: New York, NY : Franklin Watts, an imprint of Scholastic Inc., 2019. | Series: The science of... | Includes index.
Identifiers: LCCN 2018031803| ISBN 9780531131930 (library binding) | ISBN 9780531133934 (pbk.)
Subjects: LCSH: Medical technology--Juvenile literature. | Medical innovations--Juvenile literature.
Classification: LCC R855.4 .S46 2019 | DDC 610.28--dc23

All rights reserved.
Published in 2019 in the United States
by Franklin Watts
An imprint of Scholastic Inc.

Printed and bound in China.
Printed on paper from sustainable sources.
1 2 3 4 5 6 7 8 9 10 R 28 27 26 25 24 23 22 21 20 19

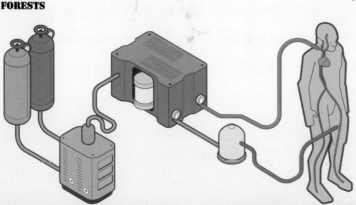

The Science of Medical Technology

From Humble Syringes to Lifesaving Robots

Written by
Cath Senker

Franklin Watts®
An Imprint of Scholastic Inc.

Contents

Introduction

Our bodies are made of many parts. On the outside are skin, hair, and nails. Our eyes, ears, nose, and mouth allow us to see, hear, smell, and eat. Inside, the bones and muscles hold up our body, and allow our arms and legs to move. Our organs do vital jobs. The brain is the control center, and the heart pumps blood around the body to keep it alive. The stomach, kidney, liver, and intestines let us digest our food to provide energy. The body is good at repairing itself when something goes wrong. If you scrape your leg or have an upset stomach, it will probably get better all by itself. Sometimes your body needs help, though. Medical technology can help find out what is wrong and cure diseases. It helps us take care of our health. Vaccines prevent people from dying from disease, and various gadgets can help us check our diet and fitness levels. If we stay healthy, we're less likely to get sick.

What Is Diagnosis?

Why It Works

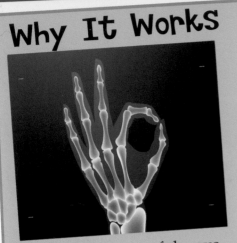

An X-ray is a powerful wave of energy that can pass through skin and muscles. Hard body parts—your bones—block the X-ray. Film behind your body captures the image made by the X-ray. The doctor can see if there are cracks in the bone.

Sometimes, a patient's regular doctor is not sure why the patient is in pain. Maybe the person had an accident and has an injury. It is best for them to go to the hospital. The doctors make a diagnosis by asking lots of questions and examining the patient. They may need to see what is happening inside the body. This is where machines can help. X-rays, and MRI and CT scanners, can look inside people's bodies and take pictures.

How Do Magnets Make Pictures?

If doctors think you might have a serious problem with your leg, they might give you a magnetic resonance imaging (MRI) scan. You place your leg in the machine, which has a large, powerful magnet around it. Radio waves are released and harmlessly hit the leg, then bounce back to the MRI scanner. A computer attached to the scanner turns the signals into images of your leg. The doctor can see if anything doesn't look right.

An endoscope is a tiny video camera on the end of a long, thin tube. It is inserted into the body to film what it sees in there.

What Is a CT Scan?

Sometimes called CAT scans, they aren't about cats! A computed tomography (CT) computer scans inside your body from different angles and puts the images together to show cross sections of all types of tissue. It's like seeing all your favorite fruits in the slices of a pie.

Can You Believe It?

What seems to be the problem? In the future, a robot doctor could be asking you this. Robots are already helping to diagnose diseases. Chatbots with speech recognition can identify patterns in the symptoms patients describe.

Can a Machine Breathe?

If the patient has been in an accident, they may find it hard to breathe. A ventilator is a breathing machine. It has a breathing tube that is put in the patient's nose or mouth. The doctor sets the ventilator to pump air with oxygen into the patient, and pump out air with waste carbon dioxide.

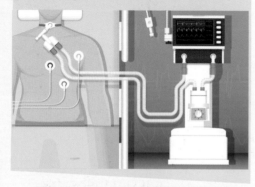

The defibrillator is an ingenious machine. It checks if a jolt to the heart is the right treatment for the patient. It won't give an electric shock if it will not help.

How Do Machines Save Lives?

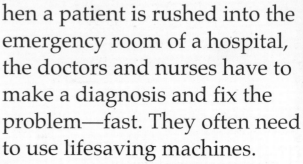

When a patient is rushed into the emergency room of a hospital, the doctors and nurses have to make a diagnosis and fix the problem—fast. They often need to use lifesaving machines.

If the patient cannot breathe, a ventilator will be used to do it for them. If the lungs aren't working, a machine can do their job. And if the heart isn't beating properly, the emergency team will try to restart it. Without these vital bodily functions, the patient could die.

Oh no, I hope whoever's inside is alright!

What Is an ECMO?

An extracorporeal membrane oxygenation (ECMO) machine does the job of the lungs, which provide oxygen to the blood cells and take away the waste products, including carbon dioxide. The ECMO pumps blood into a machine, which puts oxygen in it and returns the blood to the body.

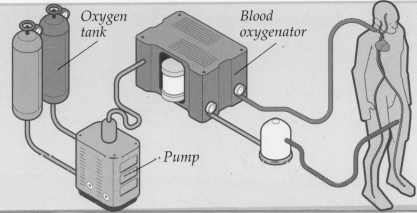

Oxygen tank

Blood oxygenator

Pump

People often think a heart attack is the same as cardiac arrest, but they are different. A heart attack is a problem with blood circulation—blood flow to the heart is blocked.

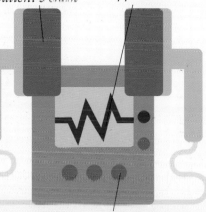

Pads to place on patient's chest

Instructions appear on screen

Buttons to trigger electric shock

How Can You Restart a Heart?

If the patient's heart is not beating normally, they may be in cardiac arrest. The heart suddenly stops pumping blood around the body. It's an electrical problem. A defibrillator sends a high-energy electric shock to the heart. The jolt can make the heart reset and start beating normally again.

Fascinating Fact

If patients lose a lot of blood, they need a blood transfusion. The new Hemosep machine gives the patient back their own blood. During an operation, the machine removes blood from the operation site, takes out the plasma (the watery part), and returns the blood to the patient. This blood recycling saves having to use blood from a donor.

Why Do Some People Need Transplants?

People may be born with an organ that does not work properly, stops working because of disease, or is injured in an accident. They need a transplant. Surgeons can transplant a kidney, liver, lung, or heart. They take out the unhealthy organ and replace it with a good one.

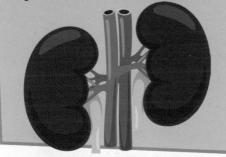

To avoid spreading germs, surgeons scrub their hands and arms before the operation and put on a face mask and gloves.

Which Machines Are Used for Operations?

Sometimes a patient might need an operation. It could be to treat an injury, replace an organ, or remove unhealthy tissue, such as cancer. In the past, if a surgeon operated on a patient's stomach, they made a cut 6 to 12 inches (15 to 30 centimeters) wide so they could see what they were doing. Nowadays, surgeons often operate on a micro scale using keyhole surgery.

Lasers can be used to treat some skin problems and eye diseases.

What Is Keyhole Surgery?

In keyhole surgery, the surgeon makes several tiny incisions (cuts) in a row. It's like cutting tiny keyholes in the patient's body. The surgeon puts a tube in each opening. Through the openings, they insert an endoscope so they can see inside the patient, and surgical instruments to perform the operation. Making tiny cuts is less risky for patients than one large cut, and they recover more quickly.

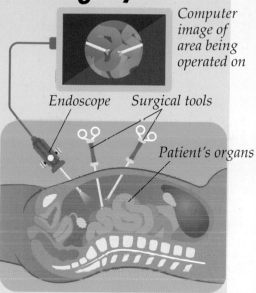

Computer image of area being operated on

Endoscope *Surgical tools*

Patient's organs

Why It Works

If someone loses a toe or finger in an accident, a surgeon may be able to reattach it using microsurgery. They use a powerful microscope to magnify the tiny blood vessels, and tiny instruments to join them together again.

How Are Lasers Used?

Lasers cut and burn. Eye surgeons use them to treat diseases of the retina at the back of the eye, and to reshape the cornea (the layer that covers the outside of the eye) of people who are nearsighted to improve their vision.

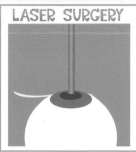

LASER SURGERY

What Is Da Vinci?

Da Vinci is a surgery robot. A human surgeon uses a computer console to control the robotic tools. The surgeon's hand movements are translated by Da Vinci into tiny movements of minute instruments inside the patient's body. An endoscope (see page 11) sends images from inside the body to a video monitor so the surgeon can see what is happening.

Live links to the operating room are great for training surgeons. Watching live surgery is much better than reading about it.

How Are Robots Used in Surgery?

Robots make great surgeons. They have a steady grip, excellent eyesight, and a huge memory for body parts and surgical methods. Robots can make highly accurate cuts—which helps healing. They are extremely good at repetitive tasks and never get tired, so they can work for hours and hours on long, complicated operations. But they still need a human to tell them what to do.

Working From Home?

The surgeon does not have to be in the operating room with the robot. They can use their computer or phone to operate a robot anywhere in the world! This way, they can assist other surgeons in real time. The advising surgeon watches a live camera feed from the operation, and marks on their device where an incision should be made.

The surgeon operating receives the image showing where to make the incision.

Could Robots Work Without Humans?

The Smart Tissue Autonomous Robot has been developed to help surgeons in the operating room. It can suture (sew up) a wound neatly and accurately.

But a human has to decide which pieces to sew together and line them up for suturing. So you won't be treated by a lone robot anytime soon.

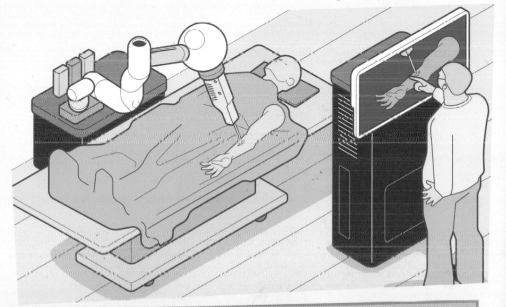

Can You Believe It?

British professor Kevin Warwick planted a microchip in his own arm, linked to the nerves that control his hand. It sends out radio signals. He can control machines with the radio signals he makes when he moves his hand. When he is online, he can operate robots in another part of the world.

How Does a Hearing Aid Work?

A hearing aid is a small device you wear in or behind your ear if you have hearing loss. When someone talks to you, the sound enters a microphone, which turns the sound waves into electrical signals. The microphone sends the signals to an amplifier, an electrical device that makes the signals stronger and sends them into your ear through a speaker. The louder sounds are easier to hear.

Some hearing aids fit right inside the ear so you cannot see them from the outside.

Which Machines Are Linked to Your Body?

Machines can mend or help body parts that don't work properly. Some are attached to the body, such as hearing aids. Others are temporarily connected to do a special job, such as a kidney dialysis machine. A few are placed inside the body, for example, pacemakers. If your grandfather has a pacemaker, he has become a bionic being—he is part machine!

Bionic man of the future?

Bionic heart

Brain implants

Bionic lungs

Bionic eye

Bionic hand

Bionic kidneys

Who Needs Dialysis?

Every living thing needs to get rid of waste substances. Your kidneys are your body's main garbage collectors. They collect extra water and waste chemicals from your blood, and you lose them through urine (pee). Some people's kidneys aren't able to do their job. This is called kidney failure. These patients are attached several times a week to a dialysis machine, which cleans their blood and returns it to their body.

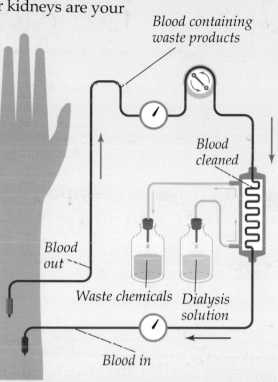

Blood containing waste products

Blood cleaned

Blood out

Waste chemicals

Dialysis solution

Blood in

What Is a Pacemaker?

A pacemaker controls the heartbeat. It has a battery and electrical circuits and goes under the skin and muscle, often near the shoulder. The pacemaker sends electrical signals to the heart through wire leads to make it beat regularly.

Pacemaker

Lead in right atrium

Lead in right ventricle

Try It Yourself

Hearing loss can have different effects. People may not be able to hear quiet sounds or high sounds, such as children's voices. When they listen to music, they may hear the low notes but not the high ones. Ask an adult to help you to try a hearing loss simulator online to find out what it is like to have hearing loss.

The heart has an electrical system that controls your heartbeat. If it doesn't work properly, you need a pacemaker.

What Are Prosthetics?

How Are Prosthetics Made?

Prosthetics are usually built from lightweight metals and strong plastics. A below-knee prosthesis has an artificial foot, a section for the missing lower leg bone, and a socket to fit onto the rest of the leg.

It's rare, but babies can be born with a missing limb (arm or leg). Or a person might lose a limb in a terrible accident or be badly injured in a war. This is where prosthetic technology can help. A prosthesis is a replacement for a missing arm or leg, and it moves in just the same way as a natural one. With a prosthetic leg, children can join in playground games and sports. In fact, they can often run faster than their classmates with flesh-and-blood legs.

Children with a prosthetic limb need to have a new one made every few years as they grow.

Can We Cure Deafness?

A cochlear implant cannot cure deafness, but it helps the patient receive some sound. The implant is fitted under the skin behind the patient's ear. It picks up sound, turns it into electrical signals, and sends them along a nerve to the brain. The brain recognizes the signals as sound.

The design for 3D printing limbs is open source, so others can use it to make a prosthesis—if they have a 3D printer handy.

How Can You Print a Hand?

A 3D printer can be used to make a limb matched precisely to a person's body. A British charity organization called Team Unlimbited makes free prosthetic arms and hands for children worldwide who are missing them. The children design the colors and patterns for their own limb.

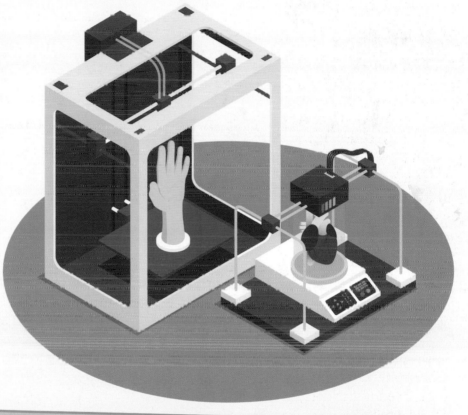

Why It Works

A 3D printer prints hundreds of 2D layers, one on top of another. The layers are bound together to form a 3D object. Imagine if you stuck every page of this book to the page before and the page after. You would have one thick 3D block instead of 32 flat pages. (Please don't try this.)

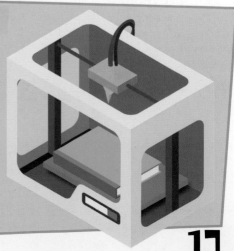

Why It Works

Vaccines are usually made from the same virus or bacteria that causes the disease. People are injected with a very weak form of the disease. It might make them feel a little ill, but they will not catch the disease. Their body's immune system makes antibodies to fight that particular disease. If the disease enters the body in the future, the immune system recognizes it, and fights it off before it does any harm.

Researchers watch out for the side effects of vaccines —effects on health that aren't intended.

What Are Vaccines?

Most drugs treat diseases, but vaccinations are a special kind of medicine to prevent people from getting sick in the first place. Vaccines can wipe out killer diseases. In 1967, around 2 million people died from smallpox. That year, a big worldwide program of vaccination began, and by 1980, smallpox had been wiped out. There are vaccines for many dangerous diseases such as polio, measles, and mumps. They provide immunity—protection from disease.

You'll just feel a pinch.

How Do Scientists Develop Vaccines?

It can take years to develop a vaccine. Scientists study the virus or bacteria that causes the disease, figuring out how it causes illness. They develop the vaccine and work out the dose needed. Will people need one shot or several? How long will they be protected for? Will people need booster shots every few years? Most of this research happens in the lab.

Once they have tried out their vaccine on a few hundred people, scientists vaccinate thousands of people around the world to check how it affects people in different places.

Who Tries Out Vaccines?

Scientists first test their vaccine on about 100 healthy adults. They check if those people's immune system kicks in to fight the disease. If the vaccine works, then it is tried on a few hundred people that it was designed for.

Fascinating Fact

When you get vaccinated, the substance has to reach the part of the body where it's needed, without causing a bad reaction. To do this, scientists figured out that vaccinations should be given in different ways. Some vaccines, such as the one for measles, are injected just below your skin and above the muscle. Others, including Hib, are injected into your muscle. The BCG vaccine goes into your skin.

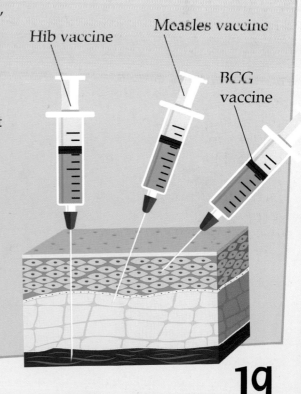

Hib vaccine

Measles vaccine

BCG vaccine

Which Vaccines Are Common?

Why Is There a New Flu Vaccine Every Year?

In the fall, you may be given this vaccine to keep you from getting the flu. Flu is a horrible disease that can leave you sick in bed for one or two weeks—that's a lot of days off from school. It is offered to people who may have trouble fighting the flu, such as older people, young children, and people with asthma. Flu is a virus that constantly mutates—changes. Vaccinations produced one year will not work the next, so scientists have to make a new vaccine every year.

W hen you were a baby, you were probably vaccinated against tetanus, whooping cough, polio, and MMR (measles, mumps, and rubella). Vaccinations are offered to everyone to stop epidemics of killer diseases. An epidemic is when a disease spreads quickly to a lot of people. Some diseases aren't normally dangerous but can be for weaker people. If nearly everyone has the vaccine, even if a few people catch it, the disease will not spread around the whole community.

Most of the world is now free of polio. There were only 22 cases reported in 2017. The only countries that still have polio are Afghanistan, Pakistan, and Nigeria.

The Measles Vaccine

Measles spreads easily when someone with the virus breathes, coughs, or sneezes. You can catch measles by being in the same room as someone who has it—even after they have left the room! Some children with measles need hospital treatment. In the most serious cases, it can cause pneumonia (a severe lung infection), brain damage, deafness, or even death. It's best to avoid the measles.

Why Do I Need Vaccinations When I Travel?

If you are traveling to a country that has dangerous diseases, such as yellow fever or typhoid, you may need special vaccinations. That's because you were not vaccinated against them when you were little.

The World Health Organization (WHO) estimates vaccines save 3 million lives a year and prevent millions of people from catching deadly diseases.

Will We Always Need Injections?

It will be several years before pill vaccines will be tested and safe to use.

Why Are Vaccines Kept in the Fridge?

Vaccines have to be kept cold because otherwise the virus used in the vaccine would die. UK scientists are working on artificial forms of the flu virus. A vaccine with an artificial virus would not have to be kept in the fridge.

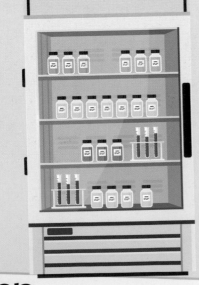

You might not like injections, but when you go for your vaccinations, you have no choice. This is because they are made with live or weakened viruses or bacteria. If you took a pill, your body would digest it before the vaccine could have an effect. Scientists are researching how to make vaccines as pills to make them cheaper and easier to give. They are also researching new vaccines for cancer and for tuberculosis—the infectious disease that kills the most people worldwide.

Hopefully we won't need to use injections forever.

Is There a Vaccine for Cancer?

Scientists are working to develop vaccines to protect against cancer and diseases that are hard to treat. Vaccines trigger the immune system to fight disease. There is hope that a cancer vaccine could recognize proteins that are on particular cancer cells. Then the immune system could attack and kill the cancer cells.

Normal cells

Cancerous cells

Scientists are working on making a single vaccine that could protect people against many diseases.

Could We Have Vaccines in a Pill?

If artificial forms of a virus were used, they wouldn't be digested by the body when they were swallowed. They could be given as pills. This would be helpful, especially in developing countries without a good electricity supply to keep the vaccinations cold. If nurses could give vaccinations without needles, vaccines would be much easier and cheaper to store, transport, and use. And it would be better for those of us with a fear of needles!

Can You Believe It?

Some US vaccine researchers wear 3D glasses and use computer graphics to see inside molecules that fight disease. A vaccine programs molecules in the body to attack an invading virus or bacteria. The body knows it has to attack the invader but it needs to find the right place on the invader's surface. It is like seeking the target in a complicated video game.

23

How Does the Nurse Check My Health?

Nurses check your blood pressure by putting a cuff on your arm and tightening it to measure the pressure when the heart is pumping and when it is resting. They check your body temperature with a thermometer. If you have a fever, your temperature will be higher than 98.6°F (37°C) and you will probably not feel very well. The nurse might need to take a blood test.

A blood test is like a vaccination, but instead of a vaccine going into your arm, the needle takes out some blood to be checked.

Which Gadgets Can Check My Health?

When you go for a checkup, the nurse and doctor have a bunch of devices to help them to examine you. Some have been around for a very long time. Doctors have been using stethoscopes since the 19th century to hear their patients' heartbeat and check that their lungs are working properly. Nowadays, all your medical records are kept on health-care computer networks so your doctor can see your medical history and look up information about drugs and diseases.

Why Do I Have to Pee Into a Bottle?

The doctor might want a urine sample if you are sick. It will be sent to the lab to be tested for infection or disease. The technician checks the color and cloudiness of your pee. They check the chemicals in it with a test strip and examine the cells and bacteria with a microscope.

Doctors ask for a urine sample to check if your body is working properly.

Which Gadgets Are Used?

The doctor uses an otoscope to look into your ear to your eardrum. It has a light and a magnifying lens. An ophthalmoscope is for looking into your eye. A light reflects off the retina (the light-sensitive part that sends messages to the brain) and back through a hole in the device. The doctor sees a magnified (larger) image of your eye.

Try It Yourself

To check your pulse, use a timer. Place the flat part of your index finger and middle finger on one side of your wrist. Press firmly but not too hard. With the other hand, start the timer. Count how many beats you feel in one minute.

How Do We Deal With Health Issues?

You, your brother, sister, or friend might have a health condition. If you have diabetes or asthma, you learn to use special devices to help you manage it. Some people have a severe allergy to nuts, eggs, or dairy products. They carry an EpiPen in case they accidentally eat something that contains that food. These devices can save their life. Even if you don't have one of these conditions, it is good to understand them so you can help others if they suddenly become sick.

What Is Diabetes?

Our cells get energy from glucose. Your body needs a substance called insulin to allow glucose into your cells. If you have Type 1 diabetes, your body does not make insulin. It tries to get rid of the glucose by making you pee a lot, and you are extremely thirsty.

People with diabetes may use a blood glucose meter to test their blood sugar level to see if it has dropped too low or risen too high.

How Do I Cope With Asthma?

Asthma affects the airways that carry air in and out of the lungs. It can make them swollen so it is hard for the air to get in and out. Breathing becomes difficult. People with asthma use a device called an inhaler, which has a reliever drug that opens the airways. They breathe it in through their mouth and it goes to their lungs to help them to breathe normally.

Possible allergies

Cheese

Eggs

Shellfish

Nuts

Strawberries

An EpiPen contains a chemical called epinephrine— also called adrenaline. It controls the allergic reaction and opens the airways to allow the person to breathe easily again.

What Is an EpiPen?

If someone has a severe allergy, for example, to peanuts, their body thinks a peanut is a poisonous alien invader and tries to fight it. Within minutes, they may find it hard to breathe. Their tongue might swell up or their skin might itch badly. To stop the reaction, they use an EpiPen injection.

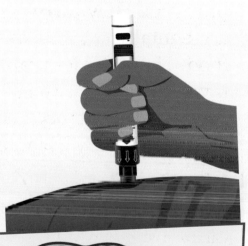

Fascinating Fact

A peanut sensor has been invented for people who are allergic to peanuts. They can carry it around to test samples of food and check if they contain any traces of the nuts.

How Do I Keep Fit?

Are you getting enough exercise? Children need at least an hour of physical activity every day, such as bicycling, running, swimming, or dancing. It keeps your heart healthy. Three times a week, you should exercise to build and strengthen your muscles and bones: Gymnastics, climbing, and soccer are great. Even computer games can keep you fit if you play the interactive dance or sports games.

If you like to swim, you can download apps with the top techniques from swimming coaches.

How Can I Stay Fit and Healthy?

e all know that we need to do some exercise every day and eat plenty of fruit and vegetables to stay healthy. But sometimes it's hard to keep track of how well you are doing. There are many gadgets and apps to help you to check your fitness and diet, and active computer games can encourage you to exercise. It is also important to make sure you have enough sleep—and there's even a gadget for that.

Good boy, Buster!

How Can I Eat Better?

We should eat at least five portions of fruit and vegetables every day to get vitamins, minerals, and fiber. Carbohydrates such as potatoes and pasta provide energy. Dairy or dairy alternatives, including milk and soy milk, have calcium to keep your bones strong. Protein from meat, fish, eggs, and beans helps you grow. A little fat is fine, but sugary foods should be only an occasional treat. To find out exactly what's in your food, you can use a scanning device. It is linked to an app that shows how much energy, protein, fat, and sugar the food contains.

Sugar

Protein

Dairy

Carbohydrates

Fruits and vegetables

Get Your Beauty Sleep

Did you know that eight- to ten-year-olds need around 10 hours of sleep a night? Much of it is deep sleep, when your breathing and heart rate slow down, and you barely move. Your body needs deep sleep to repair itself. You can wear a sleep tracker to check how long you are asleep and how much is deep sleep. If you're not sleeping enough, be sure to switch off the computer, TV, or other devices at least an hour before bedtime.

It's important to spend time away from gadgets. Put away that game console, switch off the computer, and go outside and play soccer or ride your bike. You'll feel great!

Try It Yourself

Children should walk at least 10,000 steps a day. That's 5 miles (8 kilometers), which takes about 1 hour and 40 minutes. You don't have to do it all at one time! Ask a parent if you can try a wearable device that counts your steps.

Glossary

Adrenaline A chemical produced by the body to deal with life-threatening situations.

Antibody A substance that the body produces in the blood to fight disease.

Bacteria The simplest and smallest forms of life; some bacteria cause disease.

Blood transfusion An injection of blood to a patient—usually from a donor but sometimes from the patient's own blood.

Booster shot An extra dose of a drug that is given to protect you from a disease for longer.

Carbon dioxide A gas breathed out by people and animals from the lungs.

Chatbot A computer program that can hold a conversation with a person, usually over the Internet.

Circuit The path of wires and equipment along which an electric current flows.

Diagnosis Figuring out the exact cause of an illness or a problem.

Defibrillator A machine that can control the movements of the heart muscles by giving the heart a controlled electric shock.

Digest When you digest food, it is changed into substances that your body can use.

Donor A person who gives blood or a body organ.

Endoscope A very small camera on a long thin tube that can be put into a person's body so that the parts inside can be seen.

Immune system The system in your body that produces substances to help it fight against infection and disease.

Incision A sharp cut made during a medical operation.

Intestine A long tube in the body between the stomach and the anus (bottom).

Kidney An organ in the body that removes waste products from the blood and produces urine (pee). You have two kidneys.

Microchip A very small piece of a material that carries a complicated electronic circuit.

Microsurgery The use of extremely small instruments and microscopes to carry out complicated operations on a small scale.

Molecule The smallest unit into which a substance can be divided without a change in its chemical nature. For example, if you break up a water molecule, it would no longer be water.

Nerve Any of the long threads that carry messages between the brain and parts of the body, enabling you to hear, see, and move.

Open source Used to describe computer software that is free for everyone who wants to use it.

Organ A part of the body that has a particular purpose, such as the heart or the brain.

Oxygen A gas that people and animals need to breathe to live.

Retina A layer of tissue at the back of the eye that is sensitive to light and sends signals to the brain about what is seen.

Symptom Change in your body or mind that shows you are not healthy.

Tissue A collection of cells that form the different parts of humans, animals, and plants.

Vaccine A substance that is put into the blood to protect the body from a disease.

Virus An infective agent, too small to be seen without a microscope. Some viruses cause infectious disease.

Vitamin A natural substance found in food that is important for people to eat to help them grow and stay healthy.

Index